7-STEP GUIDE TO MASTERING UNSHAKABLE SUCCESS

NERISSA MALLOY

7 Steps to Mastering Unshakable Success

Copyright © 2019 by Nerissa Malloy

All rights reserved.

Printed in the United States of America

ISBN 978-1-7339553-2-4

CONTENTS

INTRODUCTION

I created this book for the women out there who have goals and dreams but have not taken action. This is for the woman that let her self-doubt, past experiences, hurt, shame, fear of failure and fear of embarrassment, hold her back from living the life that she desires. This book is for that woman who has totally given up on herself, in order to put her family first, the woman that loves her kids and husband to death and neglects her own inner desires.

I have experienced some of these things before. I was in a space where I played it safe, stayed in the comfortable uncomfortable situations because of self-doubt. I let myself go, and I let other people's beliefs cause me to dim my light and doubt my own strength and ability. I was at a point where I let society tell me what success was instead of understanding and identifying what truly made me happy and successful. I write this book as an answer for the woman who really wants to create her own unshakable success and needs to know where to begin.

This book will give you the seven steps that I used to create success and I am sharing it with you. This book will not only help to define your success but to design your unshakable success. I pray that it gives you the ammunition you need to remove the self-doubt and limiting beliefs, take action, and create the consistency you need to push through any obstacles you may face on your journey.

I am rooting for you and believe that I am no different to any other person out there.

If I can do it, so can you!

DEFINE
"UNSHAKABLE"

When you think about "UNSHAKABLE", what typically comes to mind? Unshakable, in my opinion, is something that you strongly feel, something that you know cannot be changed or wavered. Unshakable is something that is undisputed or cannot be questioned. Can you imagine having this kind of success? A success that is undoubtedly yours and no one can take it from you. Amazing right? Well, in this book, I'm going to give you my secret sauce to achieving this level of success and becoming unshakable!

I know you're thinking "why should I even read this book or follow these steps?" Well let me share something with you. Success is not given it is earned through trials and tribulations.

I was that kid that failed consistently,

from cutting classes, teen pregnancy, gang affiliations, spousal incarceration…. should I go on? I know what it means to have hopes and dreams pulled from you. I remember in my senior year of college, receiving a letter in the mail. It was an acceptance letter from my first-choice college. I was so excited and in a few seconds of looking down at my pregnant belly, I realized, that this dream would never come true.

As I reflect on my past, I realize that these setbacks were setups for my comebacks. These lessons groomed me into the person I am today and positioned me to show others how NOT to let their failures hold them back.

ORDERING
THE STEPS

If you're reading, I suggest you carve out some time in a quiet corner. Grab a pen, highlighter and notepad and dive in to the seven steps that has allowed me to achieve "Unshakable" success and learn how you can to. *Let's dive in!*

STEP 1: Define your success.

What is success? What does success mean to you?

Success must be something of purpose and not defined by materialistic items or things that are tangible. Success must have a personal meaning to you and have an impact on others. In today's world success is about money, cars, jewelry, big houses, and likes. These things have no personal meaning and striving for tangible success leaves you unfulfilled and empty. Have you seen the recent news of all the famous and successful designers, actors etc. that committed suicide? They all were very successful, but something indeed was missing.

Success also must be defined by you and not by others. For example, often as parents, we look at the things in life we missed out on and want the same for our children. We let our mistakes and shortcomings define what success for our kids should be. In my opinion this leaves your children to accomplish goals in order to make their parents happy as opposed to defining what success means to them, defining their own personal goals towards success and striving for it.

I remember a time when I wanted my

daughter to become a nurse just like myself. She started college and wasn't doing good in science. She flunked the class and ended up dropping out. I knew she loved fashion deep in my heart but wanted her to have a solid career first. When I asked her why she started doing nursing she told me "because I wanted to make you proud". This wasn't her dream it was mine, and she lost precious time not following the path she desired. Had she the opportunity to define what success means to her, she would have an idea of what she truly wanted, created her roadmap and start moving towards her dreams.

It is so crucial that YOU understand what success means to you and then define what success is for you. This is the first step in creating unshakable success. According to Wikipedia, success is the achievement or accomplishment of an aim or purpose. Therefore, once you have achieved your goal or accomplishment then this should determine that you're a success, right? WRONG!!

The problem that is occurring today is that people are determining their success based on other people's achievements. Most often, people are looking around and comparing themselves to the success of others and using this as a measurement tool for their own success.

What I'm here to tell you is that success cannot be defined by other people. You need to determine what success is for you. We all may have similar gifts and purposes, similar journeys and testimonies, but our overall successes will not look and feel the same. We do not have the same audience, market, or followers although, some people may feel they do. God has already predetermined your audience for you to serve and impact. He has already mapped out your journey and the people you will serve. There is room for you to be successful at anything you put your mind to, therefore no one else can determine your success but you with the accountability of God.

Purpose is another key factor in achieving success. Knowing and understanding what your purpose is can help to identify and define what success means for you. You must identify why are you on this earth? Who are you here to serve? What is your story? And who needs to hear it?

When I was younger, success for me as a party promoter was having a sold-out party, driving a fancy new car, buying Gucci bags and shoes, taking trips, and more. Where I lived in Brooklyn this was success! As, I continued to seek more fulfillment and build a relationship with God, I understood that those tangible items were for folks outside to look at me and say that I am successful.

After a while the parties, shopping etc. became unfulfilling and redundant for me. It didn't have any meaning and became boring. I used to partner up with friends and have free events for kids, especially on Halloween. The free kids' parties on Halloween brought me so much joy just to see their happy faces. This brought me more joy than the actual adult parties and led me to start doing more fulfilling activities. What this later confirmed, was that, I needed to have a life of purpose.

I had to do a lot of digging deep, quiet time in prayer, reflecting and more to understand why I am here and what my purpose was. It led me to identify that my purpose is to touch the lives of young women across the world and provide them with the tools they need to define and design their own success. I understood that my success needs to be determined by my impact and I later launched my non-profit for young ladies ages 11-18 called Sweets Girlz Inc.

Spiritual gifts are something I learned of during my time of reflecting and soul searching. I took a spiritual gits assessment online and learned that my spiritual gift was leadership and administration, which helped me to understand my current advancements in my career and businesses. I advise you to make sure you go online and Google the spiritual gifts assessment and take it. The spiritual gifts test helped me to identify who and where I am to serve. Once I learned and understood my spiritual gift and who and what I was placed on this earth for, my definition of success completely changed.

As a disclaimer: spiritual gifts are deposited in you once you accept Jesus Christ as your savior. I am not forcing any religion on anyone. This is my story as a Christian and how I achieved my unshakable success. Tune into your higher power for discernment on what your attributes are and use them to achieve the success you desire.

Based on my accomplishments so far, no one can tell me without a doubt that I am successful because I am doing what I defined success was for me. This is the one thing that helped me to create unshakable success especially because I identified it and no one else did. Once you can develop this mindset and perspective on your own success, you will become unstoppable.

STEP 2: Describe what success looks like on you.

Grab your pen and paper, get in a quiet spot and answer the following questions:

When you have reached your pinnacle of success, what does your typical day look like?

1) *Who are you serving and impacting?*

2) *Where are you doing this? At home office? Overseas?*

3) *What is your dream job or business?*

4) *How do you feel when you're doing it?*

5)   *Take some time to really think about and feel this out. Write down your day from when you wake up through going to bed.*

Whether you start your day with quiet time or a shower and music, get the kids off to school, workout, head to home office etc. You are writing down what your typical day will be like once you have reached the success you desire. Take some time to envision this, write it down and don't leave any details out.

Now you have the key elements to help you feel the emotions of your success and although you may not have achieved it as yet; you have a good idea of what's possible, where you're going and how you will feel when you accomplish it.

Most often people use meditation as a

great practice to sit, be still, to receive and envision what it would feel like to achieve the success they desire.

This is a great start and a great practice. I'm going to be transparent. When I meditate and identify what success is for me, I assure you I do have some materialistic things I see for myself. This is OK because success doesn't mean that you must be broke. We know God placed us here to have an abundant life and yes abundance can mean finances as well. Therefore, when I meditate and I envision what success looks like on me, I am driving the latest white Range Rover with the butter scotch interior and I don't feel anyway guilty about it. When you think about success and your impact, just know that God will bless you abundantly. You don't have to worry about the negative things you have been told about having money, how wealthy people attain money, or that money is evil. Just understand that the LOVE of money is evil so don't feel guilty when you envision having money as being a part of your success.

Success can be financial freedom; it could be time spent with your family, just doing homework with your little one, attending recitals and games, not being stressed with the everyday commute of work or simply hosting a workshop for underprivileged youth. Success can be time spent in your ministry serving, it can be the people you coach and mentor, or your dream job or career. Whatever you're doing to make a change or make a difference in someone else's life can help you with feeling successful.

STEP 3: Change your beliefs and see how things change.

You Deserve Success! Success is your birthright. In order to achieve the success that you are destined for, you must believe that you can achieve it. Beliefs are a big key to your success and ties into your outcomes. If you believe that you won't find that good husband, that dream job, the thriving business, that child you have been longing for or that you can't lose those pounds, then it won't happen.

Unfortunately, beliefs can also be a product of your past experiences. I will never forget the time when I was voted least likely to succeed in middle school. I didn't realize how much it influenced me until I did some serious soul searching, bible reading and meditation through a discipleship class. This class allowed me to dig deep to find out my limiting beliefs and uproot them for good.

I learned that everything I did to be successful was for others to see me as a success and not for my own personal satisfaction. As I mentioned earlier, I spent money on trips, parties, expensive bags, shoes etc. just for people to believe and see me as a success. In the end, I kept searching for more. After I accepted Jesus Christ as my savior and understood the importance of having faith, I learned that your faith and beliefs, especially in yourself are critical to your self-belief and creating success.

Another important thing I learned is that your beliefs are a product of your mind and your faith is a product of your spirit. The two together are keys to driving you towards the success and fulfillment you truly deserve.

There are three things you must do and have in order to improve your beliefs about yourself and your situations.

a) First, you must BELIEVE you deserve all things great! "............Anything is possible if a person believes." Mark 9:23 NLT. I had to personally do a mindset shift in order to change my beliefs from negative ones to empowering ones. I had to stop the stinking thinking and replace it with positive, empowering thoughts but how did I do this?

I started to change what I exposed myself to by reading books for personal development, attending conferences, participating in masterminds and hiring coaches for different levels in my life. I stopped spending money on frivolous things of no value and decided to invest in myself. Personal development helped me to not only know my potential but directed me on how to work toward the success I wanted to achieve. Personal development will enhance the belief you have in yourself and your abilities.

b) Second, you must step your spiritual game up. Be intentional about your quiet time, prayers and meditation practices. Set an alarm in your phone and schedule this time daily. It can be as little as 10 minutes or an hour. You decide the amount of time you need to refuel spiritually. Find scriptures that speak to your situation and helps to build your faith.

I have scriptures in my calendar set for a specific time each day. At 8:30am my calendar reminds me of my Faith Prayer: "For I am about to do something new. See, I have already begun! Do you not see it? I will make a pathway through the wilderness. I will create rivers in the dry wasteland." Isaiah 43:19 NLT. Pick a time that works for you to not only schedule your quiet time but to also schedule your scriptures in your calendar. You can imagine how it feels when you're on the midst of something frustrating and an encouraging scripture pops up and reassures you. These 2 steps helps me to not only hold myself accountable to my daily spiritual practices but also keeps me encouraged, faithful and spiritually grounded.

c) The next step to help increase your beliefs is to **Take Action** despite your fears or beliefs. With any goals you must have your plan of action, this is your roadmap and guide to your success. Most people get stuck at this phase, the action phase. Doubt, fears and disbelief start to kick in when it's time to take action.

I remember a time I was asked to tell my story in front of a room full of women at a women's empowerment conference. The host was a millionaire, and very successful in different business ventures, and had a room full of women of all-powerful calibers yet she wanted me to share my story. I had so many doubts in my head, Why me? Why my story? I bad talked myself and must laugh as I think back. Have you ever done this to yourself?

I spoke that day and pleaded for the need for mentors for my non-profit. I did such an awesome job, that I had women coming up to me and offering their services to be mentors. That event boosted my confidence and my self-belief because I took action. Creating evidence that you are confident and empowered to achieve your dreams comes from you taking action despite your fears and doubts.

There is no straight path to success, so understand that you will have bumps and bruises along the path, but the key is to stay on path and enjoy the journey. As you continue to stay in action and stop entertaining the thought of quitting, these three key points will help to improve your self-belief and keep you focused on your defined goals. You will begin to feel more confident and motivated to continue taking the necessary steps to accomplish your goals and see your small wins.

STEP 4: The Power of Positive Self-Talk and Using Affirmations

As mentioned earlier, your mind can be your biggest enemy. There is a constant battle going on in our minds. One of my favorite bible verses is in 2 Corinthians 2:5 and it mentions that we should take captive every thought to make it obedient to Christ.

The enemy has a clever way of getting into our minds and using our negative thoughts to defeat us. The thoughts that tell you that you cannot achieve your financial goals, you are not good enough, who are you to be teaching others, who qualified you, are thoughts that can impede your progress. These thoughts cause you to shrink and not take action.

We are human and oftentimes we still have doubt. I mean honestly if you do not have a doubt then you are just not real. Every successful person faces doubts and fears, but the key is that they move despite their fears.

The key to overcome your doubt and help develop your self-talk is to choose the right set of words, phrases or affirmations that you can read and reflect upon whenever you're having a doubt. You can start out with using one affirmation or phrase that you can repeat back to yourself whenever you have a moment of doubt. One of my personal favorite phrases is "If you can get through this you can get through anything Nerissa". I often say this to myself whenever I'm in a period of struggle, doubt or pain. It helps me to confirm that God has already mapped it out and has the answer for me.

I want you to take a moment and come up with a phrase that you can use whenever you feel fearful, hopeless and doubtful. What can you to power phrase be? It must be powerful and must be something that moves you to action. Some examples of phrases may be: "I got this". "If it is to be then it's up to me". Or perhaps another personal favorite of mine is "I have the power to get through this". Think of a phrase that you can use and take a few minutes to write it down below.

____

____

Now affirmations are similar except it's not a simple phrase. Some of my affirmations are spiritually based but it doesn't have to be for you. Choose phrases that moves you to action and can be your guide. When deciding to create your powerful affirmations use these three "P's" as a guide.

a)   The first P is for **POSITIVE.** Your affirmations must be positive. You should not have an ounce of negativity in your affirmation. Do not use the words I intend to, want to, or I hope to, it must be positive and intentional. For example, "I am achieving ……. Goal". "I am a powerful being and I will touch and impact the lives of many women across the world". "I am fully equipped and capable to deliver …… service to ……. ". Make sure that your affirmations are positive.

b)   The next P is for PRESENT. Your affirmations must be in present tense, can't be anything from the past or something that will be occurring. For example, "I will accomplish", "I am doing" ……." I have all that I need to change and impact the lives of 1 million women across the country with my coaching program". It must be in the present tense so that you can see and feel it with emotions. You must be empowered by them and feel as if you are already accomplishing it. Some people feel affirmations are just wishful thinking, but I believe that if you use these positive words, ensure it has meaning, and ties to your emotions then the law of attraction will help you to achieve it.

c) The last P is for POWERFUL. Your affirmations must be positive present and powerful. Your affirmations must be of great meaning and power; something that you know you can't achieve in your own strength. Something where you must rely on a higher power to accomplish it so you can't play small with these affirmations.

A few of my affirmations are derived from bible verses. I would first list a scripture and then I would have a phrase behind it. For example, here is one of my affirmations from the prayer of Jabez in 1 Chronicles 4:10 NIV …

"Oh, that you would bless me and enlarge my territory! Let your hand be with me and keep me from harm so that I will be free from pain" *and impact the lives of many according to your will.*

When thinking about your affirmations, think about your goals, what you would like to achieve, where you see yourself in 90 days, 12 months, 2 years, and 10 years. Think about how you would feel when you achieve these goals and then write a statement to support this. Take a moment, put down the book and write out one affirmation using the three P's above.

I keep a list of affirmations in my notes folder in my phone so I can always go back, read it and reflect on it. I set a reminder in my phone every day to read them and I encourage you to be consistent with this especially in the beginning and make sure you read it every day.

Here are a few of my Affirmations that I keep in my phone to look at a couple times a week as a reminder.

1. *Today, I welcome love, joy, peace, opportunity, Energy, vitality, creativity, wealth and results.*

2.   *I am good enough to provide value and help others. I am full of energy and clarity to spill out useful and impactful content.*

3.   *I am beautiful, healthy, lean and sexy. The weight is melting off me. I have no aches and pains and I work out doing what I love*

4.   *I am FEARLESS, confident, a powerhouse and I attract those that need what I offer. I don't procrastinate - I always take massive action.*

5.   *I am wealthy and a successful investor, I own rental properties and have a positive monthly cash flow to help my family, friends and community. Money comes to me in many ways.*

6.   *I am fully equipped for Gods good works. I am an amazing mom, daughter, sister and friend. I am a passionate, energetic and loving wife.*

The power of self-talk and what we believe about ourselves influences our experience of the world. You could be going through the same thing another person is going through but because of your beliefs, and your self-talk through your affirmations, your experience through your trials can totally be different.! Now that you have created one affirmation, go ahead and create 4 more and incorporate your present powerful and positive affirmations into your daily work habits.

Take a moment and write out your four additional affirmations that you can keep in your folder and post around your room, your office space or anywhere to create positivity in your life, improve your belief and self-talk.

STEP 5: Gratitude

The power of Gratitude opens the door for continued success. Ask yourself, what are you grateful for and why? Who are you grateful for and why? Share with someone that you're grateful for them. Put this into your daily practice and acknowledge one thing or person you are grateful for. The power of gratitude and being grateful is another key factor of creating unshakable success.

You must be able to look back and be grateful for where you are and where you're going. If you can only focus on what you don't have there is no way that you will be blessed with greater. One of my favorite verses is found in Matthew 23:25 "You have been faithful with a few things; I will put you in charge of many things". This is huge for me and has played a significant factor in my growth over the last few years. I realized that if God sees that I am faithful with the few things that I am provided with now, then he will be able to trust me and bless me with more.

I want you to really take a moment to look back at all the things you're grateful for. If you must go back to your childhood take some time and really reflect from your childhood to where you are now. Do not reflect on any failures or disappointing time, I want you to really reflect on how you overcame obstacles, what you are grateful for and the lessons learned. Some things may seem minor to you, but they should all be acknowledged. Think about things that involve your family, your career, what you have been able to accomplish, how you helped someone, or touched their life.

Think of some of the simplest thing's like your career, being able to purchase this book or attend the webinar, the conference, and sometimes the people you meet and connect with. You can start out by simply being grateful for health, for your life, for your right mind, for activities of your limbs, and your family. Why are you grateful for your family? your kids? your spouse? your parents or siblings? Anyone who has great meaning to you why are you grateful for them? Think about your other connections, your friends, people you associate and do life with. Who do you fellowship with? Use this opportunity to send a thank you card or note, text or call someone and just let them know that you're grateful for them being in your life, the impact they have and what they mean to you.

I want you to really take some time and write out the people and things you're grateful for. If you have a business, you're grateful to have taken the leap to get started because most people are afraid to just to take the leap and start a business. If you're grateful for a new home you have purchased, launched a new course, even if one person signed up for that course you must be grateful for that one person and deliver like it's 1000. I find when you're grateful, you have a positive heart, you become much more humbled.

The other key piece to being grateful is to recognize and celebrate all your wins. Celebrate the things you're grateful for, the hurdles you overcame and accomplishments you made regardless of how small you may think they are.

STEP 6: Goal-Setting.

Setting goals provides the Compass to Success. It identifies what direction you're going and are important to creating unshakable success? Your goals are your roadmap. Think about this, you're about to take a road trip from New York to Florida, you're all packed up, have the kids ready, suitcases packed in the car, you have your snacks packed and gassed up to go. You start the engine and prepare to drive but you don't have GPS, a map, or the directions. Where are you going?

This is how it is with your life when you're just moving day to day and you have no goals to direct your path to success. When I speak of goals, I'm not talking about New Year's resolutions that you write in January and by March they fallen off the radar. I'm talking about actual goals that are specific, measurable, actionable, realistic and have a time frame, otherwise known as SMART goals. You may be familiar with SMART goals already and this may be a refresher, but this acronym is the key to creating goals that will lead to success.

You would be surprised to know how many people have not identified their goals. They wake up every day, take a shower, brush their teeth, get dressed, get in traffic go to work, have lunch, get back in traffic to get home, eat dinner, watch TV, go to bed and start over the next day. This is their everyday life, with no goals, desires or aspirations. They don't desire change and are just coasting day by day in the same routine. Don't let this be you, in fact if you're reading this book, I commend you because it means you are looking to break free from the rat race and the everyday mundane of doing the same thing over and over. It means that you are looking to create success, and this is a great start by reading this book.

I have a SMART goals worksheet that will show you how to write out your goals and the action steps to help you to achieve these goals. Goals are crucial in ensuring that you remain focused. For example, if you have a financial goal of saving an extra thousand dollars a month, when faced with the option of going out to eat and going over your budget you'll reflect on your goals. Your goals help you to realize that going out to eat isn't conducive to you saving that thousand dollars this month.

If you have a goal of losing a certain amount of weight when you know that you can't afford to skip your workout routine. Your goals are what keeps you focused on your achievements. The same goes for any level of success, your goals are what helps you to stay focused and gives you direction. Goals can be applied in your home, with your children, at work, ministry, business, personal, relationships and more. Make sure you have goals that you can measure and that are leading to success in all areas of your life.

When we talk about goals and goal

setting, there are three types of goals. You have your short-term goals, long-term goals, and your lifetime goals. Your short-term goals Typically range from one month to a year but mostly something that you can accomplish within a year's time frame. Whether you want to save an extra $2000 this year, launch your business or create healthier habits, these are some examples of short-term goals.

Next, you have your long-term goals which are maybe 13 months to 10 years. These goals typically take longer to achieve and are not something that you can do overnight. Purchasing a new home or buying a new car can be a long-term goal, especially if you need to start saving or cleaning up your credit. In some cases, this can take a little longer than 12 months to achieve but again there's no limit on how long a long-term goal should be. It can be two years, three years or 10 years.

Then you have your lifetime goals. Lifetime goals are generally goals you want to achieve 10 years and beyond and basically in your lifetime. One of my lifetime goals is to have my nonprofit impact 1 million girls across the world. Lifetime goals can be an overall career goal like if you want to go back to school and get your masters or PHD, save 1 million for your retirement etc.

Understanding that you have short, long and lifetime goals and that they must be SMART goals are a great way to ensure that you have the roadmap to success in your life.

STEP 7: Consistency.

This is the most lucrative step in the process of creating unshakable success. When you're consistent with something, or someone you build trust. Think about when you're consistent with your children and making sure that they have what they need, school supplies, lunch packed, school clothes, dinner cooked etc. they can trust that their mother will always be there to take care of them because of your consistency.

Think about being consistent in your career with meeting deadlines, turning in projects, following up and completing tasks. Ultimately, you'll get an increase, promotion or recognition because of your consistency and you build trust with your boss that you can be relied on.

I want you to apply this with your goals, your business, your health, spirituality and your relationships. Consistency is what helps to build trust in all those areas and with other people, but we want to focus on being consistent with yourself. If you can be consistent with your self-talk, your actions and all the other things discussed in this book, then you can trust and believe that you can achieve that unshakable success you desire.

Consistency is not just about the actions you need to take but also about your beliefs. Consistency helps you to build routines and create momentum in your life. The lack of consistency creates inefficiencies in your ability to achieve success.

Your inconsistencies leave room for the enemy to sneak in and attack your positive mindset. He will use your doubts to overcome you, causing you to procrastinate and attack your self-belief.

I see this most times in conversations with women that want to do something new but are afraid to because they haven't developed a consistent practice of overcoming their self-doubts. They also have not created the action plan to take the steps they need, and consistently take action.

Consistency requires you to be fully engaged in your actions and to be fully committed and dedicated to your goals. If you have a microwave mentality and want results quick, then your consistency will waiver as soon as you hit obstacles along your journey. The key with consistency is that although you are taking small actions over a short time that will lead to long-term success, therefore you're not looking for your success right away. You understand that by taking consistent small actions will lead to the overall big success.

Consistency with positive actions have the same effect as consistency with negative actions. Let's look at weight gain and understand that consistently snacking and overeating will cause increases weight gain over time. You will start to see the results of the weight gain when your clothes don't fit like it used to or you're tired and sluggish and develop poor health. Let's reverse this and make it a positive one about the successful people you know from Oprah Winfrey Jay Z, P Diddy, Michele Obama, Beyoncé and more. I've used these entertainers only because we've seen them grow for over 15 years at least. We have witnessed their evolution from when they started in their careers, and the action steps, they took to make them the great people they are today.

Success did not happen overnight, but you can see that they are consistent in their talents and success. Beyoncé, for me, is the ultimate example of consistency, from her Destiny's Child days and moving to becoming a solo artist. You see her consistency in her performances, concerts and music. You have seen her totally evolve in her success and you can speak to her consistency.

Consistency is not just about repetition and consistency involves personal growth as well and opportunities for you to reflect, reevaluate and re-strategize. Reflecting on your actions and evaluating if it's bringing you the results are key elements to achieving success. Learning to re-strategize if you're not getting the results, you're looking for are also critical in evaluating your consistency. Re-strategizing your action plans helps you to reset goals and stay on path to success.

These 7 tips must be in place for you to achieve the unshakable success you desire. You must be able to define it, describe it, believe it, say it, be grateful for it, set goals for it and be consistent with it.

ABOUT THE AUTHOR

Nerissa Malloy was a teen mom at age 17 and overcame all odds from being voted "least likely to succeed" and teased in middle school, to gang affiliations, wanting to feel accepted, low self-esteem, and other teen struggles. Despite all odds and graduating from high school pregnant, she pressed her way through raising a baby, working, and attending school to pursue her dreams of becoming a Registered Nurse. Nerissa later stepped into entrepreneurship where she empowers young ladies and women entrepreneurs across the world to develop the right mindset to attract and achieve the success they desire.

Nerissa resides in Maryland with her husband

and 6 kids. She founded a SweetzGirlz, a national non-profit organization, continues to work in healthcare leadership, and is an active ministry worker. She devotes her time to the community by serving on the board of Bethany Christian Services, a non-profit which serves children and families in the Maryland & D.C. region.